Animal Body Coverings

Why Do
Owls and Other
Birds Have
Feathers?

Holly Beaumont

heinemann
raintree

To contact Capstone Global Library please call 800-747-4992, or visit our web site www.capstonepub.com

Edited by Clare Lewis and Kristen Mohn
Designed by Richard Parker
Picture research by Svetlana Zhurkin
Production by Victoria Fitzgerald
Originated by Capstone Global Library

Library of Congress Cataloging-in-Publication Data
Beaumont, Holly, author.
  Why do owls and other birds have feathers? / Holly Beaumont.
    pages cm.—(Animal body coverings)
  Summary: "Find out all about feathers and how they help owls fly, keep warm, hunt and survive. Discover how feathers are different on different birds and how they change as birds grow up."— Provided by publisher.
  Includes bibliographical references and index.
  ISBN 978-1-4846-2533-0 (hb)—ISBN 978-1-4846-2538-5 (pb)—ISBN 978-1-4846-2548-4 (ebook) 1. Feathers—Juvenile literature. 2. Birds—Juvenile literature. 3. Children's questions and answers. I. Title.
  QL697.4.B43 2015
  598.147—dc23   2015000291

This book has been officially leveled by using the F&P Text Level Gradient™ Leveling System

Acknowledgments
The author and publisher are grateful to the following for permission to reproduce copyright material:
Dreamstime: Dave M. Hunt Photography, 21, 23, Jhernan124, 13; iStockphoto: summersetretrievers, 9; Newscom: Photoshot/NHPA/Joe Blossom, 17; Shutterstock: Aliaksei Hintau, back cover (right), 16, 22 (top right), Chantal de Bruijne, 7, Critterbiz, 15, Dave Montreuil, 14, Dennis W. Donohue, 11, Erni, 8, fullempty, 4 (bottom), HHsu, 23 (rabbits), Lee319, cover (top), LesPalenik, 19, Marcin Sylwia Ciesielski, 18, 22 (bottom), 23, Mark Bridger, 5, meaofoto, 20, mlorenz, cover (bottom), monticello, 4 (top right), Oleksandr Chub, 23 (velvet), PeterVrabel, 23 (peacocks), Sorapop Udomsri, 6, 23, Steve Allen, 4 (top left), TheX, 10, 22 (top left), Tomatito, back cover (left), 12, Tracy Starr (feathers), cover and throughout

We would like to thank Michael Bright for his invaluable help in the preparation of this book.

Contents

Some words are shown in bold, **like this**. You can find them in the picture glossary on page 23.

Which Animals Have Feathers?

Birds have feathers. Birds have beaks and wings. They also lay eggs.

Different birds have different types of feathers.

Owls are birds. They have large, flat faces and big eyes.

What Are Feathers?

Feathers are made from the same **material** as your skin, hair, and fingernails.

Feathers grow out of the skin of birds.

Feathers can be soft and fluffy.
They can be strong and straight.

Different feathers do different jobs.

Do Feathers Keep Birds Warm?

Feathers protect birds from chilly nights and cold winters.

Birds fluff up their feathers to trap air against their skin. This air warms up and keeps the birds warm.

This great-horned owl has lots of thick feathers.

They help it to stay warm at night.

9

How Do Feathers Help Birds Fly?

Most birds use their feathers to help them fly.

Strong wing feathers help birds take off and fly through the air. Long tail feathers help them to steer.

wing feathers

tail feathers

Owl feathers are soft and **velvety**.

They help owls to fly quietly as they hunt for food.

Do Feathers Keep Birds Dry?

Some waterbirds, such as ducks and gulls, have very waterproof feathers.

They stop the birds from getting too wet and cold.

Owls do not like flying in the rain. Their feathers are not very waterproof.

They get soggy and heavy. This makes flying hard work.

Do Feathers Help Birds Hide?

Some birds use their feathers to hide from **predators**.

This nightjar nests on the ground. Its brown feathers make it hard to see.

This snowy owl is getting ready to pounce on its **prey**.

Its white feathers make it hard to spot against the snow.

What Else Are Feathers For?

Some birds don't want to hide.

For male birds, bright feathers are a good way to get noticed.

This peacock is hoping to attract a **mate** with his colorful display.

16

Female birds are often less colorful.

This peahen needs to stay hidden while
she cares for her eggs.

How Do Feathers Change as Birds Get Older?

Many baby birds can't fly right away.

They spend their first weeks in the nest. Their soft, **downy** feathers help to keep them warm.

The young birds' wing muscles get stronger. The birds grow long flight feathers.

Soon they are ready to leave the nest and fly for the first time.

How Do Birds Take Care of Their Feathers?

Pests such as lice can eat and damage bird feathers. This can make the bird sick.

Feathers are very important to birds. They have to take care of them.

This owl is **preening**.

It is using its beak to clean its feathers. It checks the feathers for any damage.

Feathers Quiz

Which of these feathers are for keeping birds warm?

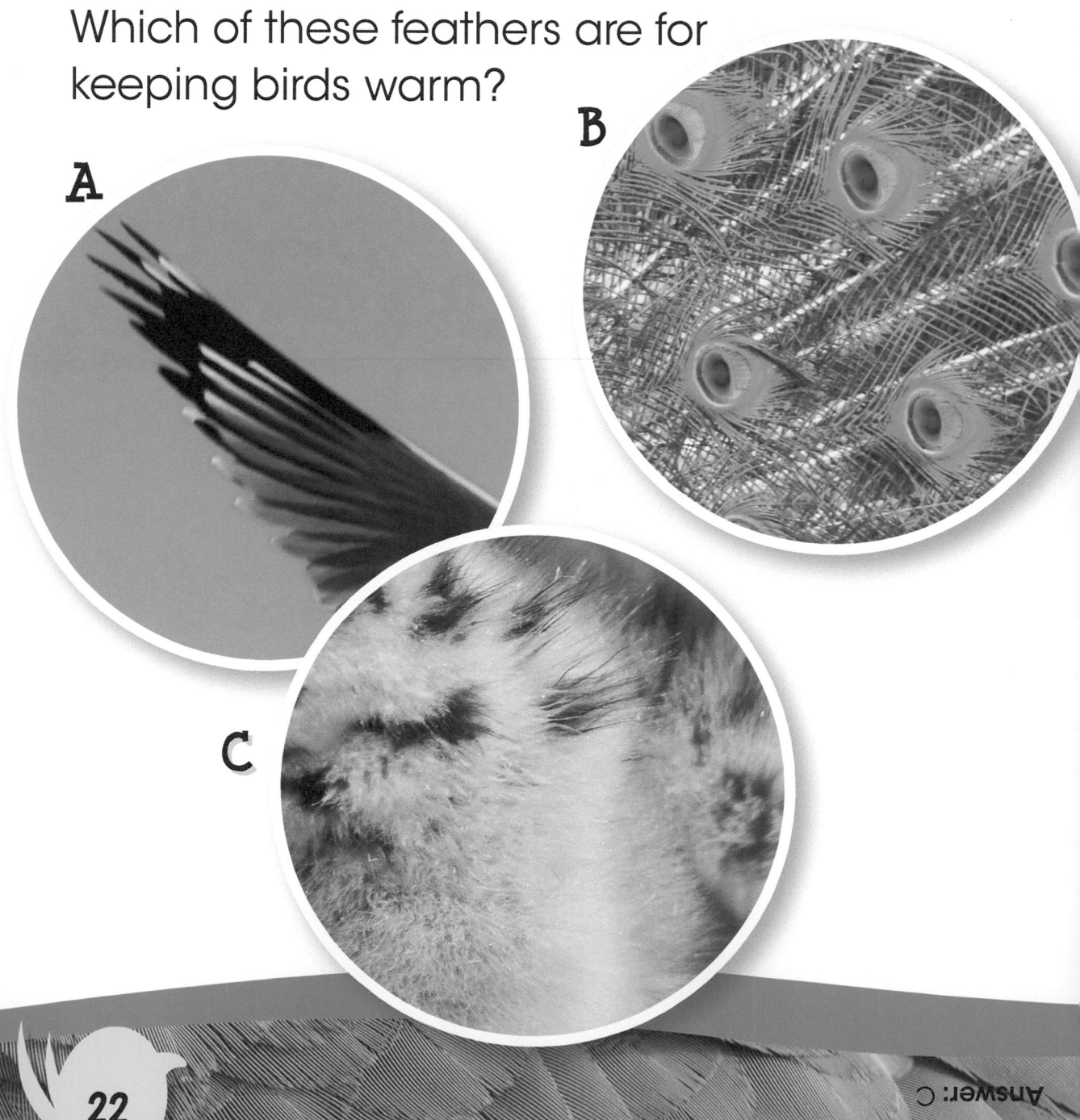

A

B

C

22

Picture Glossary

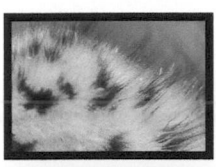 **down**   soft, fluffy feathers covering baby birds

 **mate**   male and female partners that come together to make babies

 **material**   substance from which something is made

 **predator**   animal that hunts and eats other animals

 **preen**   to clean and smooth feathers with a beak

 **prey**   animal that is hunted and eaten by another animal

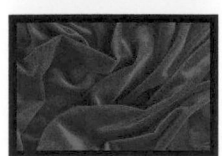 **velvety**   feeling like velvet fabric, soft to the touch

Find Out More

Web sites

Facthound offers a safe, fun way to find Internet sites related to this book. All of the sites on Facthound have been researched by our staff.

Here's all you do:

Visit *www.facthound.com*

Type in this code: 9781484625330

Books

Bodden, Valerie. *Owls* (Amazing Animals). Mankato, Minn.: Creative, 2014.

Bone, Emily. *Owls* (Usborne Beginners). New York: Scholastic, 2014

Whitehouse, Patricia. *Barn Owls* (What's Awake?). Chicago: Heinemann Library, 2010.

Index

Animal Body Coveri

Why Do
Monkeys and Other
Mammals Have
Fur?

Holly Beaumont

heinemann
raintree

To contact Capstone Global Library please call 800-747-4992, or visit our web site www.capstonepub.com

Edited by Clare Lewis and Kristen Mohn
Designed by Richard Parker
Picture research by Svetlana Zhurkin
Production by Victoria Fitzgerald
Originated by Capstone Global Library
Printed and bound in China by Leo Paper Products Ltd

19 18 17 16 15
10 9 8 7 6 5 4 3 2 1

Library of Congress Cataloging-in-Publication Data
Beaumont, Holly, author.
  Why do monkeys and other mammals have fur? / Holly Beaumont.
    pages cm.—(Animal body coverings)
  Summary: "Find out all about fur and how it helps monkeys keep warm and survive. Discover how fur can be used as camouflage, how fur is different on different mammals and how fur changes as mammals grow up."—Provided by publisher.
  Includes bibliographical references and index.
  ISBN 978-1-4846-2534-7 (hb)—ISBN 978-1-4846-2539-2 (pb)—ISBN 978-1-4846-2549-1 (ebook) 1. Fur—Juvenile literature. 2. Mammals—Juvenile literature. 3. Hair—Juvenile literature. 4. Body covering (Anatomy)—Juvenile literature. 5. Children's questions and answers. I. Title.
  QL942.B43 2016
  599.147—dc23   2015000292

This book has been officially leveled by using the F&P Text Level Gradient™ Leveling System

Acknowledgments
The author and publisher are grateful to the following for permission to reproduce copyright material: Dreamstime: Manit Larpluechai, 19; Getty Images: Visuals Unlimited/Robert Pickett, 20; Minden Pictures: Kevin Schafer, 11; Shutterstock: Alis Leonte, 16, Anan Kaewkhammul, 6 (bottom), Arto Hakola, 10, artpixelgraphy image, 13, Christian Musat, 4, 22 (bottom), Dennis W. Donohue, 6 (middle), EBFoto, 5, 22 (top right), Eduard Kyslynskyy (leopard fur), cover and throughout, Eduardo Rivero, cover (bottom), HHsu, 17, Kongsak Sumano, 12, 23, Lau Chun Kit, 21, Magdanatka, cover (top), Michael Zysman, 7 (middle left), npine, 9, ramarama, 6 (top), 23, Szilvi9, 7 (bottom), TippaPatt, back cover (left), 7 (middle right), Tom Reichner, 14, 23, Traci Law, 18, visceralimage, 8, Yongyut Kumsri, back cover (right), 7 (top), 22 (top left); SuperStock: Biosphoto, 15

We would like to thank Michael Bright for his invaluable help in the preparation of this book.

Every effort has been made to contact copyright holders of any material reproduced in this book. Any omissions will be rectified in subsequent printings if notice is given to the publisher.

All the Internet addresses (URLs) given in this book were valid at the time of going to press. However, due to the dynamic nature of the Internet, some addresses may have changed, or sites may have changed or ceased to exist since publication. While the author and publisher regret any inconvenience this may cause readers, no responsibility for any such changes can be accepted by either the author or the publisher.

Contents

Some words are shown in bold, **like this**. You can find them in the picture glossary on page 23.

Which Animals Have Fur?

Mammals have hair or fur.

Mammals are animals that give birth to live young. Mammal mothers make milk to feed their babies.

Different mammals have different types of fur.

Monkeys are mammals. They have fur over almost all of their bodies.

What Is Fur?

Fur is a thick coat of hair that grows over the body.

It is made from the same **material** as your skin and fingernails.

Fur can be long or short.

It can look
patterned
or plain.

It can feel soft and fluffy
or coarse and wiry.

What Is Fur For?

Fur is like a coat or a wool sweater. It helps to keep mammals warm.

Fur traps air next to the animal's skin. This air warms up and keeps the animal warm.

These Japanese macaques live where it is very cold and snowy.

They have long, very thick fur. They can fluff up their fur to trap more air.

Does Fur Keep Mammals Safe?

For animals that live outside all day, fur protects their skin from sunburn.

Fur also protects animals from bites, bumps, and scrapes.

This woolly monkey lives high up in the trees.

Its thick, soft fur protects it from scratches and insect stings.

Does Fur Help Mammals Hide?

Most animals have fur coats that help them blend in with their surroundings.

This tiger's striped fur helps it hide in grass. It can creep up on **prey** without being seen.

This monkey has gray and brown fur.

This helps it to hide in the trees from **predators**.

How Else Can Fur Help Mammals?

Some mammals use their fur to send a message.

When this deer is scared, it flicks its white tail. Other deer see the flash of white and know there's danger.

When this monkey is in danger, its long hair stands on end.

This makes it look bigger and helps scare away an attacker.

Are Mammals Born with Fur?

Some mammals, including monkeys, are born with thick fur.

Other mammals, like these mice, are born with no fur. Their hair starts to grow when they are a few days old.

Some mammals have only thin fur when they are born.

A mother rabbit pulls fur from her own tummy. She puts this in the nest to help keep her babies warm.

Why Does Some Fur Change Color?

This baby deer has a spotted coat that helps it stay hidden in long grasses.

As it gets older, it will lose its spots and grow a thick new coat for winter.

Leaf monkeys are born with bright orange fur.

This makes it easy for their parents to keep an eye on them.

How Do Mammals Take Care of Their Fur?

It's important for mammals to keep fur free from pests such as fleas.

Fleas are tiny biting bugs. They live and feed on the blood of larger animals, making them weak or sick.

flea

Monkeys check each other's fur for pests. They comb the fur with their fingers.

Monkeys can find it very relaxing!

Fur Quiz

Which of these images shows monkey fur?

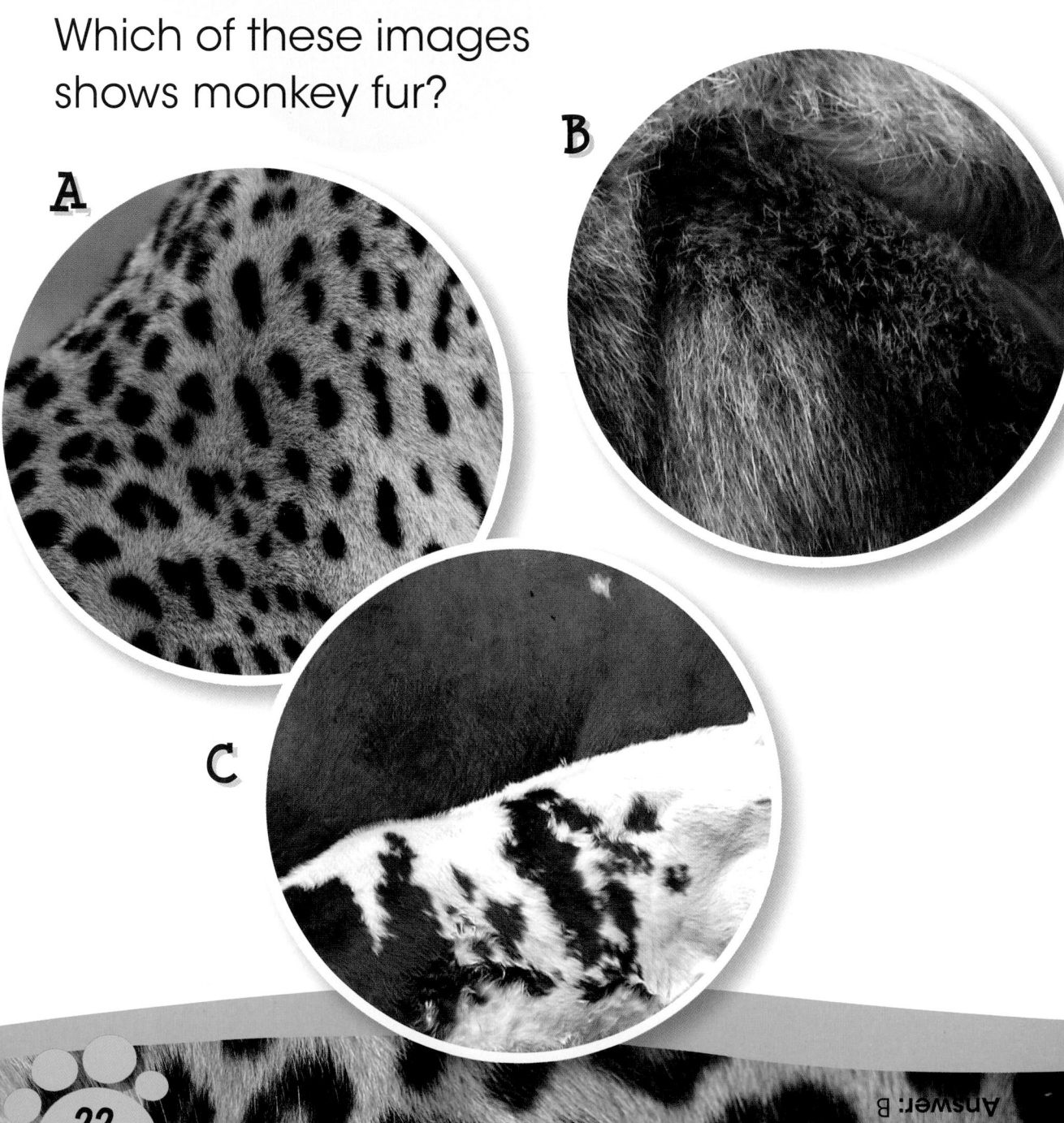

A

B

C

Answer: B

Picture Glossary

 **material** substance from which something is made

 **predator** animal that hunts and eats other animals

 **prey** animal that is hunted and eaten by predators

Find Out More

Web sites

Facthound offers a safe, fun way to find Internet sites related to this book. All of the sites on Facthound have been researched by our staff.

Here's all you do:

Visit *www.facthound.com*

Type in this code: 9781484625347

Books

Boothroyd, Jennifer. *Fur* (Body Coverings). Minneapolis: Lerner, 2012.

Thomas, Isabel. *Marvelous Mammals* (Extreme Animals). Chicago: Raintree, 2013.

Throp, Claire. *Monkeys* (Living in the Wild: Primates). Chicago: Heinemann Library, 2012.

Index